Wake Up!

Explorer Challenge

Find out who wears this
nightcap ...

OXFORD
UNIVERSITY PRESS

"It's time for bed," Mum told Biff and Chip. "Kipper's already asleep."

Chip looked at his watch. "It's a bit early, isn't it?" he said.

"We need to leave early tomorrow to drive to Gran's house," said Mum. "So we need a good night's sleep."

Soon, Biff and Chip were in their pyjamas and getting ready for bed.

"Night-night," said Mum. "I'll wake you up nice and early. Sleep well."

"You won't need to wake me up," said Chip. "I'm going to set the alarm on my new watch!"

The next morning, Chip went into Biff's room.

"Wake up, Biff," he said. "My alarm has gone off and Mum said we had to get up early."

"Hang on," Biff gasped. "It's only six o'clock."

"Oh no!" said Chip. "I set the alarm to the wrong time!"

Suddenly the key glowed. It was time for an adventure.

4

The magic took Biff and Chip to an empty street.
The sun was only just beginning to come up.

"It looks as if it's even earlier here than it was at
home," said Chip with a yawn. "I think everyone is
still asleep."

"Wait," said Biff. "*Someone* is awake. Look!"

The door of a big house had opened and a tall man was hurrying out. He was carrying a big bag and he was in such a rush that he did not even close the door behind him.

The man put his head down and began to walk quickly down the street.

"Good morning," Chip said brightly.

The man looked surprised to see anybody on the street so early in the morning. He mumbled a gruff reply as he continued on his way.

Biff scratched her head. "This is a strange adventure," she said. "What are we supposed to do when everyone is still asleep?"

Chip shrugged. "I'm not sure," he said. "Let's go that way and see if we meet someone else."

8

Soon they were passing rows and rows of smaller houses. They could hear the faint sound of snoring from behind one or two windows. They turned a corner and saw a man who was looking round in a panic.

"Hello," said Biff. "Are you OK?"

"No!" said the man. "My pocket watch is missing and I need it for my job!"

"What's your job?" asked Chip.

"I wake people up," answered the man. "It's very important."

"Don't they have alarm clocks?" asked Chip.

"No, I have the only watch in town," explained the man. "My name's Alf. It's my job to wake people up on time. If I can't do it, they will be late for work."

"Don't worry," said Biff. "We'll help you look for your watch."

"There have been a lot of burglaries lately," said Alf. "What if a burglar crept into my house during the night and stole my watch?"

"We saw a man coming out of a house with a big bag earlier on," said Chip.

"Oh no!" said Biff. "Maybe *he* was the burglar!"

Alf was getting more and more worried. "How can I wake people up on time when I don't even *know* the time?" he said.

Chip looked at his watch, but he realized that it was set to the time back home. "I don't think my watch is right," he said.

"I know!" said Biff. "Is there a clock tower near here?"
"Yes," said Alf, "there's one in the market square."
"That will give us the right time," said Biff. "Let's go!"
They ran off towards the market square.

They were out of breath when they reached the tower. Chip set his watch to the right time, but Alf looked more worried than ever.

"It's later than I thought," he said. "I don't think I'll be able to wake everyone up in time."

"We'll help you," said Biff.

They hurried to Alf's house and Alf showed the children a long bamboo pole leaning against the wall.

"This is what I use to wake people up," he explained. "I have a spare pole in the backyard that you can use."

Carrying the spare pole, the children followed Alf to
another house. He tapped gently on the upstairs window.

"Can't we just shout 'wake up' very loudly?" asked Chip.

"No, some people get angry if they are woken up by
mistake and don't get enough sleep," explained Alf. "We
have to wake up the right people."

"OK," said Biff. "You just tell us which windows to
knock on and we will do it."

Alf gave them a grateful smile. "Thank you," he said.

"Let's get going," said Biff, "so we don't run out
of time."

They had to be quick, so Alf pointed out some houses and the children ran to tap on the windows. They could hear people waking up inside.

"It's working," said Chip.

They ran from street to street, tapping on all the windows that Alf pointed out to them.

19

They were running out of time. Eventually they reached the last street.

"We did it!" Biff said, with a grin. She reached up to tap on the last window.

"Wait!" hissed Chip. "Alf didn't tell us to do that window!"

But it was too late.

"Oi!" shouted a gruff, angry voice from behind the window. Then the window opened and a man stuck his head out. "What are you playing at?" he yelled. "Some people are trying to get some sleep here!"

"Sorry!" said Biff.

As soon as the man closed the window, Chip turned to Biff. "Did you see that man?" he whispered. "That was the man we saw earlier. I think he's the burglar!"

"What?" said Alf. "We'd better send for the police right away!"

Ten minutes later, the police arrived.

Biff, Chip and Alf waited outside the house. Then they watched as the door opened and the burglar was led away.

"Well done," one of the police officers said to the children. "There's a lot of stolen stuff in there."

"Did you find a pocket watch?" asked Alf.

The policeman shook his head. "Sorry," he said. "No pocket watch."

Alf looked glumly at the children. "What now?" he said. "Without my watch, I will lose my job! What am I going to do?"

24

Chip was about to give his watch to Alf when Biff heard a faint noise.

"Hold on," she said. "Can you hear that? It sounds like ... ticking!"

"I can hear it too," said Chip. "It's coming from the back of your jacket, Alf!"

Alf took off his jacket and checked it.

"My watch is here!" he said. "It must have fallen through a hole in my pocket into the lining of my jacket. Thank you!"

"No problem," said Biff. The key was glowing in her hand. It was time to leave.

When they arrived home, they could hear Mum calling, "Time to get up, children."

Dad came past Biff's room. "Come on," he said. "We need to leave soon. Hurry up and get dressed, please."

Fifteen minutes later, everyone was in the car. Biff yawned.

"Are you OK?" asked Mum. "Didn't you get enough sleep?"

"I'm just not awake yet," said Biff.

"Me neither," said Chip. He gave Biff a quick wink and then he yawned, too.

When they were on the motorway, Kipper wanted to play a game.

"The first person to see a yellow car gets one point," he said. "OK?"

There was no answer. Kipper looked at his brother and sister and began to laugh. They were both fast asleep.

Retell the Story

Look at the pictures and retell the story in your own words.

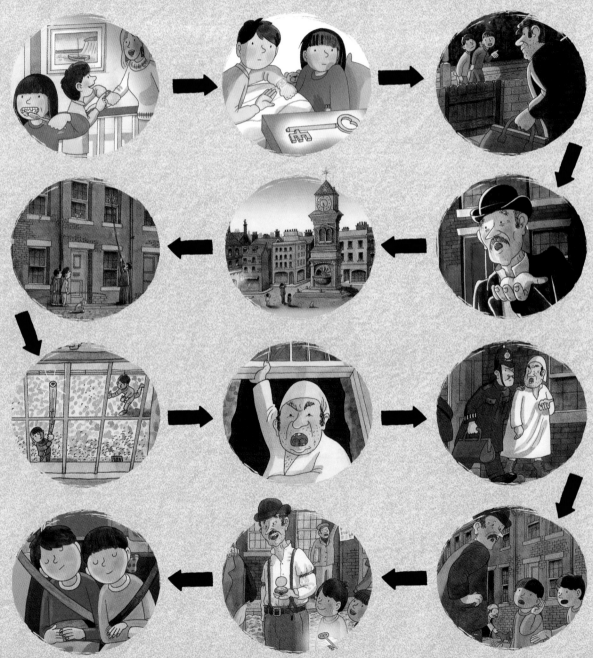

Look Back, Explorers

The burglar spoke in a *gruff* voice. What does the word *gruff* mean?

How does Alf wake people up?

Where was Alf's watch?

What might have happened if Biff and Chip had not helped Alf?

Why did Biff and Chip fall asleep in the car?

Did you find out who wore this night cap?

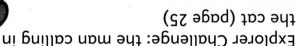

Explorer Challenge: the man calling in the cat (page 25)

What's Next, Explorers?

Now you've read about how Biff and Chip helped to wake up people on a magic key adventure, read all about why sleep is so important ...

Explorer Challenge
for *Sleep*

Find out why bats sleep upside down ...